Gofors & Grumps

Book two

G-L

An A-Z of Bible Characters by **Derek Prime**

with illustrations by **Ruth Goodridge**

DayOnepublications

Copyright © Derek Prime 1995
First printed 1995

ISBN 0 902548 58 1

Published by Day One Publications
6 Sherman Road, Bromley, Kent BR1 3JH

Designed by Steve Devane and printed by Clifford Frost Ltd, Wimbledon SW19 2SE

Gofors & Grumps

G-L

DayOnepublications

Mr **Grateful**

Something to do

Mark the map!
Find Samaria and Galilee on the map on page 39 and write in their names.

Mr. Grateful met Jesus when He was travelling between Samaria and Galilee on His way to Jerusalem.

As Jesus went into a village ten sad men met Him. They were miserable because they all had leprosy. Leprosy was a dreadful disease. It started with a little spot, and then it ate away at a person's hands or legs until perhaps only a stump was left.

Lepers were not allowed to live with their families and friends because they might pass the disease on to them.

As lepers went down the street, they had to cry out, 'Unclean! Unclean!' meaning 'Don't come near me!' They had to live with other lepers or on their own.

The ten lepers had heard that Jesus healed people. When they saw Him, they stood at a distance, and called out as loud as they could, 'Jesus, Master, have pity on us!' And He did!

As soon as Jesus saw them, He understood how ill and sad they were. 'Go and show yourselves to the priests,' He said. Priests were the people who had to decide whether or not lepers had been healed of their leprosy.

The lepers did what Jesus told them, and as soon as they went on their way, their leprosy disappeared. They looked at their skin, and nothing

Can you draw?

Draw the nine lepers going home in the distance, and the one returning to say 'Thank you' to Jesus.

was wrong with it any longer! How excited they were! Perhaps they pinched themselves to make sure they were not dreaming!

One of them was not a Jew like the others, but a man from Samaria. When he saw that he was healed, he came back to Jesus, praising God in a loud voice. He fell flat on the ground in front of Jesus and thanked Him.

The Lord Jesus asked, 'Didn't I heal ten men? Where are the other nine? Was no one found to return and give praise to God except this foreigner?' Then Jesus said to the Samaritan, 'Stand up and go home; your faith has made you well.'

Ten lepers were made better but only one came back and said 'Thank you' and that was Mr. Grateful.

Gratitude is remembering to say 'Thank you'. Do you write 'Thank you' letters? There are times when most of us do that, and especially, of course, at our birthdays and at Christmas when there are

6

presents for which to be grateful.

Some people are quick to say 'Thank you'. A lady arrived by train at a London station. The first thing she did when she got off the train was to go to the train driver and say 'Thank you' to him for a safe and comfortable journey. He was very surprised, but pleased!

To whom do we say 'Thank you' most? Yes, to our parents and our friends, and to all who help us or do things for us.

Most of all, it is right to say 'Thank you' to God for sending the Lord Jesus to be our Saviour. We can never thank the Lord Jesus enough for dying for us.

Mr. Grateful, the healed leper, came back and said 'Thank you'. One of the reasons we go to church every Sunday is to tell God in our hymns, songs and prayers, how grateful we are to Him.

We show we are grateful to people by doing things for them in return, and by serving them. We show our gratitude to God too by serving Him

Nine lepers went home without saying 'Thank you', but one was grateful and he went back to Jesus and said so.

Are we like the nine or are we like Mr. Grateful? Are we ungrateful or grateful people? Is there someone to whom we should say 'Thank you' today? Do we need to say 'Thank you' to God for something special?

Most important of all, have we ever said 'Thank you' to God for His gift of the Lord Jesus to be our Saviour?

Psalm 103, verse 2, tells us, 'Praise the Lord, O my soul, and forget not all his benefits.'

Where to read: Luke 17:11-19

Mr **Humble**

Mr. Humble is the name we may give to a man the Lord Jesus spoke about in one of His stories. I wonder how you would describe a humble person? It is quite difficult, and perhaps it is easier to think of opposites.

The opposite of humble is proud. Proud people have big opinions of themselves, and humble people do not.

Perhaps you are good at Language or Maths, or at playing football or netball. If you are good at any of these things, you may be either proud or humble about it.

Proud people talk a lot about themselves. Humble people keep quiet about themselves. Proud people want others to know how much better or cleverer they are. They like comparing themselves with others.

Humble people do the opposite. They do not draw attention to themselves, and they do not enjoy comparing themselves with other people.

Let us listen to Jesus' story, and see if you can tell which of the two men Jesus talked about was Mr. Humble.

Two men went up to the Temple in Jerusalem to pray: one was a very religious person, called a Pharisee, and the other was someone not liked very much because he was a tax-collector.

The Temple

The Temple was the special place in Jerusalem where the Jews worshipped God. The first Temple was built by King Solomon, and he followed the instructions God had given to his father, David. It was destroyed twice by invading armies and then rebuilt again. At the time of the Lord Jesus' ministry it was being rebuilt. The Temple was one of the wonders of the world. It was made of white marble, and was covered with a thin layer of gold. In AD 70 the Temple was destroyed again - this time by the Romans - and it has not been rebuilt.

Place a 'T' where true, and a 'F' where false against these sentences:

Humble people talk a lot about themselves.

Proud people think they are important.

Humble people are glad when others do well.

Proud people are quick to admit their mistakes.

The Pharisee stood up and prayed about himself: 'God,' he said, 'I thank You that I am not like all other men - robbers, evil-doers, adulterers - or even like this tax-collector. I go without food twice a week and give You a tenth of everything I earn.'

But the tax-collector stood at a distance. He would not even look up to heaven, but beat upon his chest with sorrow, and prayed, 'God be merciful to me, a sinner.'

Who was Mr. Proud? And who was Mr. Humble? The Pharisee was Mr. Proud, and the tax-collector was Mr. Humble.

The Lord Jesus said that Mr. Proud went home unforgiven. He had not really been praying at all. Instead of praying, he had been talking to himself and any around him who may have been listening. But Mr. Humble went home with all his sins completely forgiven by God.

The Bible tells us something about God which we always need to remember: 'God opposes the proud but gives grace to the humble.'

After telling His story, the Lord Jesus said, 'Everyone who thinks too much of himself will become a nobody, and whoever humbles himself will become a somebody.'

All the time we are proud, we cannot receive God's forgiveness for our sins. That was why the Pharisee went home unforgiven. If we are proud, God is not pleased with us, just as He was not pleased with the Pharisee.

The Pharisee thought God was pleased with him because he went often to church, prayed many prayers, and gave some of his money to God. But much more important to God was whether or not

the Pharisee was humble before Him and others.

The Lord Jesus, God's Son, who told this story, is the most wonderful Person who has ever lived in this world. Although so important He was never proud. He treated everyone with respect, and He kept on surprising His disciples by how humble He was, especially as one day He washed their feet, and later even went to the Cross to die in their place.

If you met Mr. Proud and Mr. Humble, which of them would you choose to be your friend? I think you would pick Mr. Humble, because proud people are never attractive.

The Lord Jesus wants all His followers to remember His example and to walk in in His footsteps. That is an important secret of being humble.

Where to read: Luke 18:9-14

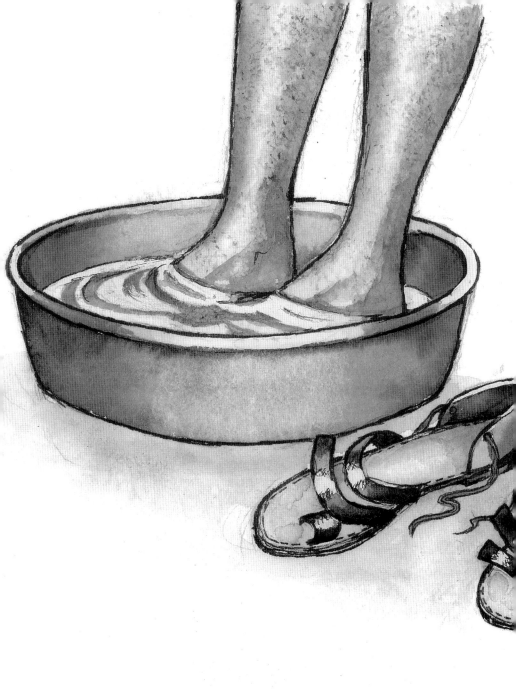

Miss **Industrious**

I hope you like learning new words. I wonder if you know what the word 'industrious' means? If anyone says you are industrious, it means that you work well and always do your best. It is a way of praising or congratulating you.

I expect your school has open evenings when your parents can go and talk to your teachers about you. Some schools give children reports to take home at the end of term or the school year. If your teachers say you are industrious, your parents will be pleased because it means you work hard. We cannot all be near the top of the class, but we can all do our best.

Miss Industrious lived in a small harbour town called Joppa on the coast of Israel. Its modern name is Jaffa, and it is just north of the city of Tel Aviv, which you will easily find on a map of Israel.

Her real name was Dorcas, a Greek word meaning 'a gazelle'. A 'gazelle' is a wild animal found in parts of Africa and Asia, and it looks like a deer.

The Bible tells us two important things about Dorcas: she was a follower of the Lord Jesus, and she was always helping others.

Dorcas heard the good news about the Lord Jesus' death for us, and how He rose again to be the Saviour and Lord of all who trust in Him. She trusted in Him as her Saviour, and she wanted to

Something to do

Mark the map!
Find Joppa, Jaffa and Tel Aviv on the map on page 39 and write in their names.

14

A disciple
A disciple is someone who wants to be taught by a teacher, and so it was a good name for the first followers of the Lord Jesus, and for all today who follow Him. His disciples are those who trust Him as their Saviour and live as He tells them to do. A disciple is another name for a Christian.

live to please Him. True disciples like Dorcas listen to what the Lord Jesus says, and obey Him.

The Lord Jesus taught that if we love Him, we will love one another. The way we behave and care for others shows whether or not we belong to Him. The way Dorcas lived showed that she belonged to the Lord Jesus.

I do not know if she had much money, but she was always doing good and helping the poor. We do not have to be rich to help others, because there are things we may do to help people with our time and energy.

One of the things Dorcas loved doing was making clothes for those who could not afford to buy them. If she heard of a widow, or a boy or girl who did not have a father, she got out her needle and thread, and made shirts and coats to fit them exactly. As soon as she finished one thing for one person, she would find something else to do for

another.

Everyone who knew Dorcas loved her. She was so kind and thoughtful.

You can imagine how sad everyone was when one day they heard that Dorcas was ill. The sadness became all the greater when Dorcas died. Everyone who knew her was upset, and many cried. Some of her friends washed her body and prepared it for the funeral, and placed it in a room upstairs in her house.

But then someone said, 'Isn't Peter staying in Lydda?' Lydda was not far from Joppa. 'And didn't Peter heal Aeneas there, who had been bedridden for eight years? Let's send a message to Peter and get him to come to Joppa to see if he can help us.'

So they sent two men to Peter, with the message, 'Please hurry and come to us.'

Peter went with them at once, and when he arrived in Joppa he was taken to the upstairs room where Dorcas was. All the widows whom Dorcas had helped stood around him, and they pointed to the clothes they were wearing which Dorcas had made. They told him how industrious she had been for them, and in all her service for the Lord Jesus.

Peter asked them all to leave the room. He knelt down and prayed to God in the name of the Lord Jesus. Then he turned to Dorcas, and said, 'Dorcas, get up!' She opened her eyes, and when she saw Peter she sat up. Peter took her by the hand and helped her to her feet.

He called in all the Christians and the widows who had been so upset, and showed them she was now alive again. Their sadness was turned to happiness! They thanked God because they knew it

Something to do

Mark the map!
Find Lydda on the map on page 39 and write in its name.

Can you draw?

Draw the widows and children showing Peter the things Dorcas had made for them.

A Christian

People who believe in the Lord Jesus were first called Christians as a nick-name. Christians are those who belong to the Lord Jesus because they know that He died for their sins and rose again to be their Saviour and Lord. It is another name for those who follow the Lord Jesus.

was not Peter's own power that had restored Dorcas to life, but the power of the Lord Jesus, in whose name Peter had prayed.

The news about Dorcas spread all over Joppa, and many people believed in the Lord Jesus. And Dorcas went on being industrious for the Lord Jesus as she continued to do good and help the poor.

What about us? Are we industrious or lazy? It is easy to be lazy at school, and not to work hard. It is also easy not to be bothered about helping other people, especially the lonely and those who are ill. When we believe in the Lord Jesus, and receive Him as our Saviour, something happens deep inside us. The Lord Jesus comes to live within us by His Spirit, and He teaches and helps us to be

kind and thoughtful to others, and to work hard at it - to be industrious.

The Bible says, 'Whatever you do, work at it with all your heart, as working for the Lord, not for men'. We cannot all be clever, and we cannot all be rich, but we can all work hard at helping others.

In lots of churches in the world Dorcas clubs or societies have been formed, named after Miss Industrious. The members commit themselves to doing kind and useful things to help others. Without joining a Dorcas club or society, with God's help we can all be like her.

Where to read: Acts 9:32-43; Colossians 3:23

Mr **Jealous**

Are you ever jealous? It is not something we like to admit, but it may often show in our actions.

Are jealous people attractive? No, they are not!

The Mr. Jealous I want us to think about was a king. Now we would not think that a king would need to be jealous of anyone, but this king was.

Mr. Jealous' real name was Saul, and he was the first king of Israel. He was very tall and strong. But I am sorry to say that he became jealous of someone much younger than himself, a young man called David.

Saul had not always been jealous of David. When he first met him, he liked him and soon grew to love him. He first admired David when he volunteered to fight against Goliath when everyone else was afraid to do so. He saw David run out to met Goliath, and watched as he hurled one small stone from his shepherd's sling at Goliath's head with deadly accuracy.

Saul ought to have liked David all the more when he became the best friend of Jonathan, Saul's son.

Whatever Saul gave David to do, he did well. It was not long before Saul made him commander of all his troops.

But David's great success in battles soon made

Saul jealous. When Saul and David came home from war, the women came out from all the towns of Israel to cheer. They sang and danced for joy, and played their tambourines and other musical instruments. As they danced, they sang: 'Saul has killed his thousands, and David his tens of thousands.'

Saul was angry when he heard this. 'For David they claim tens of thousands,' he thought, 'but me with only thousands. The next thing they will be wanting is for David to be their king.'

The Bible says that 'from that time on Saul kept a jealous eye on David'. Jealousy made him do lots of silly and stupid things. First, it made him angry, and when we let ourselves get angry, we may do things we are sorry about afterwards.

One day David was playing his harp for Saul, as he often did. Suddenly Saul threw his spear at David, but missed. This happened at least two other times.

In the end Saul decided he would try to get rid of David. First, he thought he would give David a dangerous battle to fight against his country's enemies, the Philistines, so that they might kill him. But his plan failed.

Saul then told his son Jonathan and all his servants to kill David, but Jonathan warned David so that he escaped.

Sometimes Saul realised that his jealousy was wrong, and he then promised not to hurt David any more. But soon his jealousy became so strong again that he broke his promises.

God did not let Saul capture David. God is never pleased when we are jealous.

I wonder if we are sometimes jealous? It can happen on other people's birthdays. When they open their presents, we may be jealous of the gifts they receive. Or perhaps our friends play the piano or football better than we do, and instead of being glad we find fault with them, because deep down we are jealous.

Someone may have a friend whom we would like to have as our friend, and we may be nasty to that person because we are jealous.

Jealousy took control of Saul's life because he did not listen to God. Once upon a time God had been with Saul in all that he did, and helped him, just as He helped David. But in the end God left Saul all alone and stopped helping him, and his jealousy then just got worse and worse. The Bible says that jealousy is even more horrible than anger.

How can we stop being jealous? To begin with, there are things we need to know about jealousy.

Jealousy is something Satan, the devil, loves to

Our Bible dictionary

Prayer

Prayer is talking to God, and is part of the special relationship we have with God when we trust in the Lord Jesus as our Saviour and come to God in His Name. Prayer is asking God for the things that we know He wants for others and ourselves. In what we call the Lord's Prayer, the Lord Jesus teaches us the kind of things we should ask God for when we pray. See Matthew 5:9-13. God wants us to talk to Him about everything that worries or concerns us.

see in us because it makes us like him.

Jealousy is sin, and is one of the things for which the Lord Jesus Christ had to accept the punishment we deserve when He died on the Cross so that we could be forgiven.

When we become Christians, jealousy belongs to the way we used to behave before we were Christians, and not to the way we now want to live as the Lord Jesus' disciples.

There are two things we can do to help us overcome jealousy. First, we can pray for the people of whom we are jealous, asking God to help us to love them and to care about them. Then instead of being jealous of their birthday presents, we will be glad that they are pleased with the gifts they receive. Rather than criticising them, we will

24

True or False?

Place a 'T' where true, and a 'F' where false against these sentences:

If we are jealous we will be cross when others do better than we do.

If we are jealous we will be quick to congratulate others when they succeed.

If we are jealous people will want us as as their friend.

praise and encourage them.

The second thing we can do is to ask God to help us to be happy with what we have. We do not need to be jealous of other people. God made us as we are with our own gifts and abilities. When we add up all the good things He gives us each day, we realise how stupid we are to envy what other people have.

Where to read: 1 Samuel 18:1-17; Proverbs 27:4

Mr Kindness

Something to do

Mark the map!
Find where Samaria, Jerusalem and Jericho are on the map on page 39 and write in their names if you have not done so already.

Do you remember?

The Temple
Please turn to page 9 if you have forgotten!

I wonder how you would describe a kind person? Can you think of someone who is kind? He or she will be thoughtful, generous and always willing to help you.

Kind people put others before themselves. I cannot tell you the name of the Mr. Kindness we are going to think about, although I know he came from Samaria. The Lord Jesus told a story about his kindness.

A man was going down from Jerusalem to Jericho, when he fell into the hands of robbers. They stripped him of his clothes, beat him and went away, leaving the poor man half-dead, lying in the road.

It so happened that a priest was going down the same road, and when he saw the man, he passed by on the other side.

So too, a man who helped in the Temple in Jerusalem, called a Levite, came to the place, saw the wounded man, but passed by on the other side, just like the priest.

But a Samaritan, as he travelled along the same road, came to where the man was. When he saw him, he felt very sorry for him. He went up to him, and cleaned and bandaged his cuts and bruises.

Then he put the man on his own donkey, brought him to a place where travellers might

Draw the Samaritan helping the man who fell into the hands of robbers. You might like to draw the priest and the Levite in the distance, walking away.

spend the night. and cared for him. The next day he took out two silver coins and gave them to the owner of the place. 'Look after him, please,' he said, 'and when I return, I will pay the bill for any extra expense you may have had.'

Which of those three men deserves to be called Mr. Kindness? Yes, the Samaritan. He was thoughtful, helpful, and generous. He put the poor injured man's needs before his own business.

The kindest person who has ever lived in this world is our Lord Jesus. He went about doing kind things. He was so kind that He even died on the Cross for us, to make it possible for our sins to be forgiven. When we trust Him as our Saviour we want to be like Him, and that helps to make us kind.

There is a story about two brothers, one of whom had a family and the other had none. They both sowed a field of wheat. On the evening after

28

the beginning of the harvest, the older brother said to his wife, 'My younger brother is unable to bear the heat and work of the day as I am; I will get up, take some of my sheaves and place them with his without his knowing.'

The younger brother had the same kind thought. He said to himself, 'My older brother has a family, and I have none. I will get up, take some of my sheaves and put them with his.'

Imagine how surprised they were the next day when they saw that their stacks of sheaves were more or less exactly the same, in spite of what they had done!

This happened for several nights. Then each decided to keep guard and solve the mystery. They did so, and to their surprise met each other half-way between their piles of sheaves with their arms full! They were being kind to one another, and they had not wanted to show off about it.

A boy from a poor family went into a butcher's for his mother. As he was leaving, the man who owned the shop said, 'Have you got a dog at home?' He gave the boy a big bag as large as the boy's head.

When his mother opened the scraps, she said, 'You've picked up somebody else's parcel.'

'No,' he said, 'I didn't. He put it right into my hands.'

'But it is all little chunks of good red meat,' his mother said. 'He did not intend it for the dog at all. Everybody is so kind to us!'

Kindness is love and thoughtfulness in action. Can you think of ways in which you can be kind?

Perhaps new children join your class at school. It is kind to show them round, and include them in your games. Teachers usually know the thoughtful children whom they may best ask to look after someone new.

To show kindness to others is something which always pleases the Lord Jesus.

Where to read: Luke 10:25-37

Mrs **L**aughter

Can you laugh? I am sure you can! There are different kinds of laughter. We laugh at funny stories and jokes. We laugh when something happy or exciting happens, or when we play games with our friends.

Some laughter can be unkind. People may laugh at someone who is in difficulty, or who perhaps looks ugly or is strangely dressed. Laughter like that is cruel.

Sometimes we laugh, and cannot stop laughing! A girl, called Molly, went to school in Glasgow. One day the teacher went out of the class during an art lesson, and she left the children to draw an orange with their crayons.

The girl next to Molly had a tiny tube filled with 'hundreds and thousands', those little coloured sugar dots, no bigger than a pinhead, that are used for putting on the top of cakes. They had stuck together, and refused to come out of the tube, however hard she sucked.

Trying to help her, Molly hit the bottom of the tube sharply, and the whole lot shot out in a wet blob, and landed right in the middle of her drawing.

As they watched, the coloured sugar began to run, and in a minute the orange looked as if it had a horrible disease!

They dared not touch it in case they got it all over their clothes, and they knew the teacher would be furious with them for spoiling the page in their drawing book.

They looked at one another and burst into peals of laughter which they simply could not control. The girls in the back row crowded round to see what they were laughing at.

They held their sides, and explained what had happened between bursts of giggles. It was infectious and soon the whole class was laughing.

Suddenly the door opened, and the teacher walked in. 'What is the meaning of this?' she demanded. The rest of the class fell silent but Molly and her neighbour could not stop laughing. Tears of laughter fell down their cheeks. They shook, and their voices squeaked as they tried to speak. That was the first time Molly really got into trouble at school!

Let me tell you about Mrs. Laughter, whose

laughter was very different and secret - or so she thought!

Have you ever had unexpected visitors at home? Abraham and Sarah did. The Lord Himself appeared to Abraham near Mamre while Abraham was sitting at the entrance to his tent during the hottest part of the day.

Something to do

Mark the map!
Find where Mamre is on the map on page 39 and write in its name.

Abraham looked up, and saw three men standing close by. It was the Lord and two companions. When Abraham saw them, he sprang up, and ran to welcome them.

Abraham said, 'Sirs, please don't pass my home by without stopping. I'll be pleased to get you some water, so you may wash your feet and rest under this tree.'

Then he added, 'Let me get you something to eat, so you can be refreshed and then go on your way.'

'Very well,' they answered, 'do as you say.'

So Abraham hurried into the tent to Sarah.

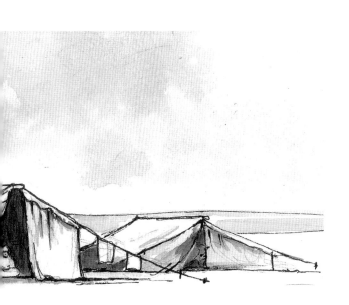

Can you draw?

A picture of Abraham looking after his guests and talking with them, with Sarah listening at the door of the tent.

'Quick,' he said, 'we've got visitors. Please bake some fresh bread for them.'

Then he ran to his herd and picked out a calf that was tender and fat, and gave it to a servant, who hurried to get it ready. After a little while he brought some cream and milk, and the meat that had been cooked, and set them before his guests. While they ate, Abraham stood near them under a tree, ready to get anything they needed.

Now Sarah, Abraham's wife, had no children. It made her very sad. Ever since she had married Abraham she had looked forward to having a family of her own, especially as God had promised to make Abraham's family grow until it would be too large to count. But the years passed and still Sarah had not had a baby.

When Abraham was a hundred years old, and Sarah ninety, God promised Abraham, 'I will bless Sarah and will give you a son by her.'

Abraham laughed with joy and astonishment, and God repeated his promise, 'Sarah will bear you a son by this time next year.'

It was soon afterwards that this visit of the Lord to Abraham took place. Abraham had told Sarah what God had promised, but Sarah had not believed it possible because they were so old.

While Abraham's guests were eating their meal, they said to Abraham, 'Where is your wife, Sarah?'

'She is there in the tent,' he replied.

Then the Lord said to Abraham, 'Next year I will give Sarah and you a son.'

Now Sarah was listening at the door to the tent. Do you know what she did? She laughed! She laughed to herself, and said, 'That's impossible! I'm too old to have a baby!'

Sarah was not only Mrs. Laughter, she was also Mrs. Listener!

Her laugh was a laugh of unbelief. She did not believe what God said.

But it was also a laugh to herself. She thought no one knew about her secret laugh.

The Lord said to Abraham, 'Why did Sarah laugh and say, "Will I really have a child now that I am old?" Is anything too hard for the Lord? Just as I told you Sarah will have a son next year.'

Sarah was afraid and she lied and said, 'I did not laugh.'

But the Lord, who knows everything, said, 'Yes, you did laugh.'

What do you think happened the following

A question

How old was Abraham and how old was Sarah when Isaac was born?

year? At the time God promised, Sarah had a baby son, and she then laughed with joy. I wonder if you can guess what Sarah said? 'God has brought me laughter,' she said, 'and everyone who hears about this will laugh with me.' Then she added, 'Who would have dreamed that I would ever have a baby at my age, and give Abraham a baby in his old age?'

But here is another question. What do you think Sarah called her son? She called him Isaac which means 'Laughter'!

Every time Sarah used his name, she remembered God's kindness to her, and how He had made her laugh with joy even though she had laughed because she had not thought God's promise possible.

Sarah discovered that God can do the impossible! Nothing is too hard for Him.

When God tells us wonderful things in His Book, the Bible, do we laugh secretly, not believing them to be possible? Or do we believe what God says?

The most wonderful promise God makes is that He will forgive us our sins and prepare a home in heaven for us if we trust in His Son, the Lord Jesus, who died for sinners on the Cross.

Do you believe that promise? If you believe it, God will fill your life with joy, and with laughter of the right kind!

Where to read: Genesis 18:1-15; Genesis 21:1-8

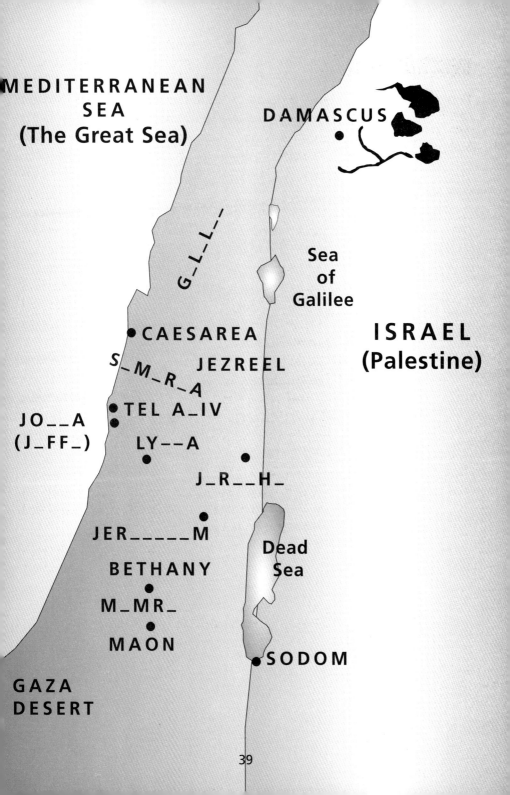

MEDITERRANEAN
SEA
(The Great Sea)

DAMASCUS

G_L_L__

Sea
of
Galilee

ISRAEL
(Palestine)

CAESAREA

JEZREEL

S_M_R_A

JO__A
(J_FF_)

TEL A_IV

LY--A

J_R__H_

JER_____M

Dead
Sea

BETHANY

M_MR_

MAON

SODOM

GAZA
DESERT

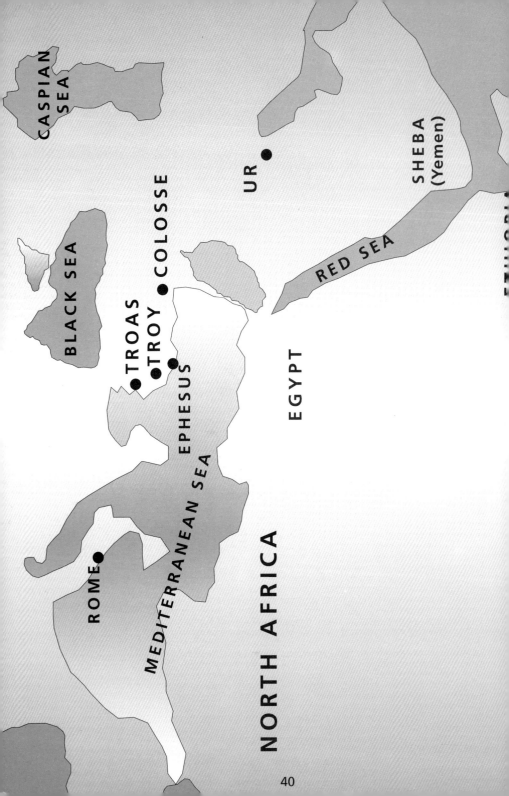

CASPIAN SEA

BLACK SEA

UR

SHEBA (Yemen)

RED SEA

TROAS

TROY

COLOSSE

EPHESUS

EGYPT

MEDITERRANEAN SEA

ROME

NORTH AFRICA